Cooking with Love

Cooking with Love

Joan Bunting

with photographs by
Paul Dodds

Bridge Studios
Northumberland
1992

Bridge Studios,
Kirklands,
The Old Vicarage,
Scremerston,
Berwick upon Tweed,
Northumberland TD15 2RB.

Tel: 0289 302658/330274

Newcastle Chronicle &
Journal Limited
Thomson House,
Groat Market,
Newcastle upon Tyne,
NE1 1ED

Tel: 091 232 7500

ISBN 1 872010 80 6

Typeset by EMS Phototypesetting, Berwick upon Tweed.

CONTENTS

To Mum, and all mums who pass on the joy of sharing
good food cooked with love

INTRODUCTION

A meal cooked with thought and care is an act of love. There are many occasions in any year to celebrate, but the love of family, friends and good food is reason enough. There is, too, something infinitely reassuring in the rhythm of the seasons, which previous generations respected and appreciated. Not for them strawberries in December and turkey in June; the produce of each season was recognised at the appropriate time with traditional recipes.

The best food in the world is still fresh, seasonal and uncomplicated. This does not always mean that it will be quick to prepare, but then the eating should be lingered over too. It will certainly be cheaper and of better quality than ready-made dishes. Complicated, 'over-wrought' food is the province of pretentious restaurants, but attractive presentation and an eye for colour are a must. After all, food is appreciated first by the eyes.

I have a theory that one of the main reasons for the demise of family life in recent times is the advent of convenience food and, more particularly, the huge increase in take-away food shops.

These days, people seem to graze rather than eat, and the sight of every other person on the street consuming food or drink is not attractive. Family meals around the table seem to be confined to a few celebrations, with Christmas being the most notable. Even then, much of the food consumed is bought ready prepared and is therefore very expensive.

Changing life-styles and, for many, more money, mean that we can buy ready-prepared food. This in turn means that many of the skills and recipes which our parents and grandparents had are disappearing.

It is still perfectly possible to lead a busy life while appreciating the traditions associated with family food. I know from the readers of my weekly column in *The Journal* that many people just need a quick reminder of how things used to be to encourage them to try a recipe for themselves. Given a few new ideas there is no holding them!

In order to cook the recipes in this book you will not require great culinary skills but you *will* need a few basic items of kitchen equipment, the most important of which is at least one good sharp knife. The ingredients are generally straight forward and if anything is out of the ordinary I have made suggestions as to where it may be found.

Above all, food is for sharing, and I hope that the seasonal ideas in the book will inspire you to do just that with family and friends throughout the year. Have fun!

All recipes will serve four people unless otherwise stated. Remember too, not to mix metric and imperial measurements; stick to one.

Coeur à la crème with passion fruit sauce (see page 16)

Spring

There is nothing so reassuring, after a long winter, to see the first signs of spring. The early snowdrops in the garden and the first of the forced rhubarb in the shops mean that the days are growing perceptibly longer and the cooking year has begun.

I view February with a mixture of emotions. There are so many traditional celebrations involving food from February onwards. I hate, however, to see the commercial element which has crept in over the years: Valentine cards and heart-shaped everything in the shops as soon as the Christmas decorations are down, to be followed immediately by Easter eggs and hot cross buns.

Valentine's Day is a very personal celebration. The best reason in the world for cooking a special meal is to celebrate romance, and we all know where the route to any man's heart lies. Most women feel exactly the same. It is lovely to be taken out to a smart restaurant, but sometimes even more romantic to stay put and enjoy a simple meal for two at home.

As Valentine's Day often coincides with Pancake Day, or near enough, it is quite possible to combine two celebrations into one.

Another nice touch is to make at least some of the food heart-shaped. Whatever you decide, keep it simple so as not to waste precious time slaving over a hot stove.

Hot cross buns (see page 22)

11

BASIC CRÊPES MIXTURE

8oz/225g fine plain flour
1 level tbsp caster sugar
3 eggs
15 fl oz/420ml milk
2 tbsp melted butter
2 tbsp cognac

Sift together the flour, sugar and a pinch of salt.
Beat the eggs and add them to the dry ingredients. Mix in the milk, melted butter and cognac gradually to avoid lumps.
Strain through a fine sieve and allow the batter to stand for at least two hours. The batter should resemble thin cream.
Heat a heavy pan and grease lightly with an oil soaked pad of kitchen paper. Add two tablespoons of batter and swirl to cover the pan. Cook on one side until the bubbles stop popping, then flip over and cook on the other side. A perfect crêpe is wafer-thin with a lacy edge. The butter in the batter gives this effect, so there is no need to over-oil the pan.
At this point it is worth a word about pancake pans. The perfect pan is quite small, with a base of about 6 inches, and is heavy: cast iron or stainless steel, with a non-stick coating if you prefer. It should also be shallow to make tossing easier. My faithful pancake pan came from a French market, but I have recently seen suitable pans in several large stores.
Once you have found your perfect pan it is better not to wash it after use, and to keep it exclusively for pancakes. After use, a quick wipe with an oiled paper towel, then store it inside a plastic bag for cleanliness.

MORELLO CHERRY AND RUM PANCAKE FILLING

1 jar Morello cherries (these are less sweet than black cherries)
1 rounded dsp arrowroot
piece of cinnamon stick
2 tbsp dark rum
thick cream or yoghurt to serve

Drain the cherries, reserving the juice. For perfection, stone the cherries, otherwise play 'tinker, tailor'!

Mix the arrowroot with a little of the cherry juice until smooth, then make up to half a pint/250 ml with the rest.

Add the cinnamon and bring to the boil over a medium heat, stirring all the time. When thickened, add the cherries and the rum and heat through.

Remove the cinnamon stick and serve inside hot crêpes or pancakes, folding them into quarters and sprinkled with icing sugar.

CRÊPES SUZETTE

I know it is sometimes not considered to be 'in' to serve flambé dishes, but I have never met with any complaints when I serve Crêpes Suzette.

½ basic crêpes mixture
4 oz/120g unsalted butter
2 tbsp icing sugar
1 tbsp grated lemon peel
juice and grated rind of one orange
6 tbsp Cointreau
4 tbsp cognac

Cream together the butter and sugar; add the grated lemon and orange rind and the orange juice. Add 4 tbsp Cointreau or other orange liqueur.

Make the crêpes and stack as described above.

To serve, heat the orange flavour butter in a deep frying pan for about five minutes.

Dip each crêpe into the butter, fold into four to form a triangle and push to one side of the pan.

When all the crêpes are done, sprinkle with a little sugar and add the remaining Cointreau with the cognac. Tip the pan towards the flame or ignite with a match. Spoon the flaming liquid over the crêpes and, as soon as the flames die down, serve.

Pancakes have always been a part of the American culinary tradition, indeed the Indians there were first with pancakes made from flour ground from acorns and beechnuts.

The American pancake is by and large a breakfast food. Fluffy griddle cakes, flapjacks 'johnny cakes' and plain ordinary pancakes are still the highlight of many an American Sunday breakfast. Served with real maple syrup and butter they are utterly delicious though I did draw the line at pancakes with bacon and maple syrup. Do serve them with real maple syrup and not that awful maple flavour stuff.

AMERICAN BREAKFAST PANCAKES

5 oz/170 g plain flour
pinch salt
1 level tbsp sugar
1 level tsp baking powder
3 eggs
15 fl oz/425 ml milk
4 tbsp melted butter

Sift flour, salt, sugar and baking powder into a mixing bowl. Separate the eggs and beat the yolks into the dry ingredients. Add the milk and melted butter and mix well.
Beat the egg whites until stiff and fold into the pancake batter.
Heat a griddle or heavy pan and when hot, drop the batter, a good spoonful at a time, onto it. When the bubbles have subsided, turn the pancake and cook until brown. Serve with butter, maple syrup and, for true authenticity, bacon and sausage.

AVOCADO HEARTS WITH PRAWN FILLING AND RASPBERRY VINAIGRETTE

1 ripe avocado pear
4 oz/120 g cooked shelled prawns
1 small carton cottage cheese
2 teaspoons chopped fresh herbs

Vinaigrette
2 tbsp raspberry purée, made from frozen raspberries
1 tbsp raspberry vinegar, or wine vinegar
8 tbsp grapeseed oil
salt and pepper

First make the vinaigrette by mixing together the purée and the vinegar. Season, then add the oil and whisk well. Chill until needed.
Reserve four prawns to garnish. Place the rest in a food processor or blender with the cottage cheese, herbs and seasoning and whizz until blended but not too smooth.
Peel the avocado pears, cut in half and remove the stone. Using a knife, cut the broad end of the avocado so that the halves look heart shaped. Fill the cavity with the prawn mixture and place them, filled side down, on two plates. Pour some of the vinaigrette around the avocado halves and garnish the plate with two prawns arranged to form a heart.

BARBARY DUCK BREASTS WITH HONEY

Barbary duck breasts are available fresh in some supermarkets. They are particularly delicious, but ordinary duck breasts would do almost as well.

2 Barbary duck breasts
2 tbsp runny honey
4 tbsp stock
4 tbsp red wine
salt and pepper
1 tbsp melted butter or oil

Brush the duck skin with the honey and season well.

Heat the butter in a frying pan and, when it is foaming, add the duck breasts, skin side down. Cook until the skin is golden brown then turn and continue to cook until done to taste. They are best still slightly pink, don't over-cook or they will be tough.

Remove from the pan and keep warm.

Add the wine to the pan juices and stir well, incorporating all the 'goodies'. Add the stock and reduce a little.

Slice the duck breasts and arrange in a fan on a warm plate. Pour the sauce around and garnish with a little heart-shaped potato cake, made by pressing finely grated raw potato into a heart-shaped metal pastry cutter in a hot frying pan containing oil. When the first is shaped, carefully remove the cutter and shape another.

Cook until crisp on one side, then turn and cook on the other. Drain well and serve very hot.

COEUR À LA CRÈME WITH PASSION FRUIT SAUCE

Traditionally, for this following French recipe, you need white china heart-shaped moulds which have drainage holes in the base. They are available in better kitchen departments and shops, but I found that heart-shaped individual tins with holes pierced in the base work just as well.

1 carton fromage frais
1 tbsp caster sugar
3 stiffly beaten egg white, use free range.

Line the moulds with some muslin or an old napkin.

Drain the fromage frais very well then add the sugar and the egg white. Fold together, then fill the moulds. Place in the fridge and leave for as long as possible, at least two or three hours.

Passion fruit sauce
4 passion fruit
1 tbsp icing sugar
2 tbsp sweet white wine or 1 tbsp Cointreau

Cut the passion fruit in half and scoop out the flesh. Put this in a nylon sieve set over a bowl and drain to remove the seeds. Add the sugar and the wine or Cointreau.
Pour the sauce on to two plates.
Turn out a coeur à la creme and, if you feel very wicked, cover each with whipped cream.
Decorate the plate with some sliced fruit or some sliced strawberries.

Carlins and Beyond

An old North East rhyme which names the Sundays leading to Easter goes:

"Tid, Mid, Miseray,
Carlin, Palm and Pace Egg Day."

The third and mid-lent Sundays are followed by Passion Sunday (Miseray or Carlin Sunday) and Palm Sunday. Finally we have our Easter or Pace Eggs on Easter Sunday.
Why Carlin Sunday? In 1644 the Scots laid seige to Newcastle and the inhabitants were on the point of starvation. A French ship, carrying a cargo of maple peas managed to sail up the Tyne and the peas were distributed to the local people on Passion Sunday.
Locally these peas are called carlins and it became customary for them to be served, usually free in inns since then. Elsewhere in the country maple peas are used as pigeon feed, and here lies a coincidence. We spent several years working in the West Indies and here the staple food is a dish called Peas 'n' Rice. It is made from the very same peas, only there they are called Pigeon Peas!

CARLINS

8 oz/250 g carlins (maple peas)
water
1 oz/30 gm butter
2 oz/60 g soft brown sugar
dark rum

Wash the carlins well and soak in water overnight. Drain and cook in unsalted water until tender but not mushy. A pressure cooker greatly speeds up this process.

Melt the butter in a large pan, add the drained carlins and fry gently for 2 or 3 minutes.

Remove from the heat, stir in the sugar and sprinkle with a dash of rum. Serve hot.

PEAS 'N' RICE

1 cup carlins (pigeon/maple peas) or black eye peas
1½ cups rice
1 tbsp cooking oil
1 large onion, chopped
1 cup canned or fresh chopped tomatoes
pinch dried thyme
water
salt and pepper
dash of Tabasco or hot chilli sauce

Soak and cook the peas as described in the previous recipe; do not over-cook them.

Fry the chopped onion in the oil until soft. Add the washed rice and stir until every grain has been coated with oil.

Add 3 cups water, the peas and the rest of the ingredients, stir well.

Cover and cook until the rice is tender, adding a little more water if necessary. The rice should be moist but separate.

This is a good-natured dish which reheats well and makes a good dish for a crowd, to accompany a curry or a casserole.

PAN HAGGERTY

No book which includes any reference to the traditions of North Eastern cooking can possibly neglect a real gem. While in the olden days Pan Haggerty was served as a cheap dish on Monday, I find that it is a real winner with guests from foreign parts, like London!

2 lbs/1 kg floury potatoes, peeled
1 lb/500 g onions
4 oz/250 g Cheddar cheese

Slice the potatoes and onions.
Melt 1 or 2 tbsp beef dripping in a large heavy frying pan. The dripping is traditional, but you could use another fat or oil.
Arrange the potatoes and onions in layers, seasoning each layer.
Cover and cook until the vegetables are tender. Sprinkle with cheese then brown under the grill or in the oven and serve very hot cut in wedges.

Mothering Sunday

Once Valentine's Day is over the shops immediately begin to exhort us not to forget Mother's Day.
The real significance of this festival is said to have come from an early church tradition of visiting one's mother church on the middle Sunday in Lent. Children who lived away from home, especially girls in service, were allowed to return to their families and took with them a specially baked cake.
We know this cake as a simnel cake and these days it is better known as an Easter cake. It is pleasant to revive the old custom, however, and it certainly makes a good alternative to over-priced flowers.
Another way to pamper mother on this special day would be by making her a really special breakfast. I like nothing better than to have a really luxurious breakfast cooked for me, and I guarantee that I am not alone.

SIMNEL CAKE

8 oz/250 g plain flour
pinch salt
Large pinch baking powder
2 oz/60 g rice flour
8 oz/250 g sultanas
4 oz/125 g currants
4 oz/125 g glacé cherries, halved
1 oz/30 g candied peel, chopped
8 oz/250 g butter
Grated rinds of 2 lemons
8 oz/250 g caster sugar
4 eggs, separated
Beaten egg to glaze
1 lb/500 g marzipan
A little glacé icing

Line an 8 inch/20 cm round cake tin with non-stick paper.
Set the oven to gas mark 4/180°C/350°F.
Sift the flour with the salt, the baking powder and the rice flour into a large mixing bowl.
Mix together the prepared fruit.
Cream the butter with the lemon rind until it is soft, then add the sugar and beat until light and fluffy. Beat in the egg yolks.
Whisk the egg whites until firm. Fold one third of the sifted flour into the mixture, then fold in the egg white alternating with the rest of the flour and the fruit. Do not over-mix.
Put half the mixture into the prepared tin. Take a little less than half the marzipan and roll it into a circle, slightly smaller than the diameter of the tin. Place this circle on the mixture, then add the remaining mixture, smoothing over the top.
Bake in the pre-set oven for 2 hours, then reduce the heat by half, and continue cooking until the cake is firm to the touch. You can't use the skewer test on this cake because of the marzipan.
Allow the cake to cool, then remove it from the tin and place on a baking sheet.

To decorate for Mothering Sunday:
Shape the remaining marzipan into a number of even sized balls and place

them around the top of the cake. Tie a band of greaseproof paper around the side to hold them in place. Brush the marzipan with beaten egg and bake the cake in a moderate oven until the marzipan is brown. When the cake has cooled, remove the greaseproof paper and fill the centre with some glacé icing and decorate with sugar flowers.

To decorate for Easter:
Take about half the remaining marzipan and roll out a circle the size of the cake. Cut a smaller circle out of the centre with a large pastry cutter to form a ring. Lift this on to the cake and crimp the edge with thumb and finger.
Take the remaining marzipan and form eleven oval-shaped balls. Place these on the marzipan ring. They represent the twelve apostles, minus Judas. Brush with egg and glaze as described above. This time, decorate with miniature eggs and a chicken.

SMOKED SALMON KEDGEREE

6 oz/175 g fresh salmon, cooked and flaked
2 oz/50 g smoked salmon cut into fine strips
6 oz/170 g Basmati rice, cooked and drained
1 onion finely chopped
2 hard-boiled eggs
2 oz/60 g butter
salt, pepper and a little cayenne
snipped chives to garnish

Fry the onion in a little of the butter until soft.
Chop the eggs and add with the rice and fish to the pan.
Season very well, add the rest of the butter and, if you like a rich finish, a little double cream.
Turn into a warm shallow dish, and garnish with a little extra smoked salmon and the snipped chives.

Easter

In most European countries, Easter is marked with cakes made from yeast doughs. In this country we make hot cross buns for Good Friday. This treat is spoilt these days by their appearance, along with chocolate Easter eggs, in the shops shortly after Christmas. Why on earth can't we wait until the proper time to enjoy things?

When my husband celebrated his 50th birthday, he asked for a 'real family lunch'. He invited twenty family and close friends and we all sat down to a meal which lasted well past tea-time.

In France and Italy such a meal is a much more common occurence, perhaps because there are still large extended families with plenty of willing hands. Easter is a perfect time to share a large, relaxed family meal, using easily cooked recipes which have been well planned in advance.

It is wonderful to share the kitchen with family and friends as you prepare such a feast, and the atmosphere, when everyone sits down together, could never be matched in a restaurant.

HOT CROSS BUNS

I know some people shy away from cooking with yeast, but a good thing about modern ingredients is the advent of 'easy blend' dried yeast. This takes the hassle out of finding fresh yeast, and eliminates the uncertainty about its freshness and the difficulty of measuring quantities accurately.

1 tbsp 'easy blend' yeast
8 fl oz/250 ml warm milk
1 lb/450 g strong plain flour
½ tsp salt
1 tsp ground mixed spice
1 tsp cinnamon
2 eggs
2 oz/60 g butter
2 oz/60 g raisins
2 oz/60 g chopped mixed peel

pastry for crosses (optional)
1 tbsp butter
2 tbsp flour
1 tsp cold water
Glaze: 2 tbsp milk mixed with 1 tbsp sugar.

Into a large mixing bowl sift together the flour, salt, sugar and spices, then mix in the dried yeast. Make a well in the centre and add the milk, melted butter and beaten eggs. Using your fingers, or an electric mixer, blend the flour into the liquid, continuing until all the flour is incorporated. The mixture will be quite soft.
Turn it out on to a well floured board, and knead until the dough is smooth and elastic, adding more flour if necessary. This will take about ten minutes, so don't worry if it seems very sticky at first.
Rinse out the bowl, dry it and grease lightly. When the dough is ready, put it back into the prepared bowl, cover with plastic film or a damp tea towel and leave in a warm place until the dough has risen and almost doubled in bulk. Punch the dough and turn it out on to a floured board. Knead it lightly, working in the dried fruit.
Preheat the oven to gas mark 8/230°C/450°F.
Divide the dough into 16 equal sized pieces and shape into buns. Place these on two greased baking sheets, cover and leave to rise again until the buns are again doubled in bulk.
To make the crosses, you can just make knife cuts on top of the buns. Alternatively, make a rich paste by rubbing the butter into the flour and mixing with water. Roll out thinly and cut into thin strips divided into 2 inch/5 cm lengths.
Press two of these on to the top of the risen buns in the form of a cross, then brush with the milk glaze before baking in the pre-heated oven for 15 minutes, or until well risen and golden brown.

AVOCADO EGG MAYONNAISE

It seems very appropriate to serve eggs as a first course for Easter. This recipe is a Jewish one reminding us that many religions have a spring celebration.
Serves 6-8

6-8 hard boiled eggs
5 fl oz/150 ml mayonnaise
1 large or 2 medium ripe avocado pears
3 tsp lemon juice
half clove garlic, peeled
pinch cayenne pepper or a dash of Tabasco sauce
salt and white pepper
To garnish; a little shredded lettuce, or Chinese leaf
cherry tomatoes
black olives
fresh parsley or chervil sprigs

The best hard-boiled eggs are very fresh, free range eggs cooked for 8 minutes in boiling water, then IMMEDIATELY plunged into cold water. This way the eggs will not be rubbery or have unsightly black rings around the yolks. Peel the avocados and cut them into chunks. Place them and the other ingredients, apart from the eggs, in a blender or food processor and blend until very smooth.
Just before serving, arrange the salad leaves, tomatoes and olives on small plates. Cut the eggs in half and place on the leaves. Coat with the avocado mixture and garnish with parsley or chervil.

CREAMY SALMON MOUSSE

12 oz/300 g fresh salmon steak
8 fl oz/250 ml milk
1 small bay leaf
6 peppercorns
slice onion
3 oz/90 g butter
1 tbsp flour
salt
2 tbsp double cream, lightly whipped
1 tbsp medium sherry

Cook the salmon in the oven or microwave, in a little water or, better still, white wine, until just cooked through. Drain the fish and dry on kitchen paper and remove all skin and bone.

Put the milk into a small pan and add the bay leaf, peppercorns, and onion. Bring to the boil, leave for a little while and then strain.

Put one tbsp of butter into a pan and, when melted, add the flour and stir well. Add the milk a little at a time, season and stir over a low heat until thickened. Turn on to a plate to cool.

Cream the remaining butter and whip the cream. Put the salmon into a food processor and blend until smooth. If you do not have a processor, then work in a bowl with the wooden spoon until the fibres have broken down.

Add the cooled sauce and the butter and check the seasoning. Fold in the cream and the sherry. Turn into a mould or soufflé dish, smooth the top and chill until needed.

Either turn out or decorate the top of the dish with sliced cucumber, and serve with a cucumber salad and some melba toast.

HONEY GLAZED NORTHUMBRIAN DUCK

A Northumbrian Duck is an absolutely perfect dish for Easter. Not duck at all, it is a boned shoulder of lamb with the knuckle bone left in and cut to represent the neck, head and beak of a duck. It is a speciality of W. G. Lough's in Jesmond and has been a favourite of customers for many years. The same cooking method can be applied to an ordinary shoulder. Ask your butcher to leave long ends on the trussing strings so that you can open up the 'duck' or the shoulder to put in the stuffing.

1 Northumbrian Duck or a boned shoulder of local lamb
3 tbsp runny honey

Stuffing
6 oz/150 g fresh breadcrumbs
3 tbsp suet
2 tbsp ready-to-eat dried apricots
1 tbsp chopped parsley
2 tbsp blanched, chopped almonds
1 egg, beaten
salt and pepper

Mix together the dry stuffing ingredients and bind together with the beaten egg.

Open up the trussing strings of the lamb and spread the stuffing on the meat. Draw up the strings and secure well.

Cover the 'duck' head with foil to prevent burning and place the lamb in a roasting tin.

Spread the meat with the honey and season well. Roast in a moderately hot oven at gas mark 5/190°C/375°F for 25 minutes per lb for medium done meat. Adjust the time accordingly if you prefer well done or pinker meat.

Remove from the oven and allow to rest for 30 minutes before carving. Serve on a 'sea' of mange tout peas or green beans with minted new potatoes served separately.

Make your gravy by adding a tbsp of flour to the roasting pan and stirring well to incorporate all the 'goodies'. Add a splash of red wine and stock or water to make a gravy of the thickness you prefer. Gravy is a *very* personal preference. My son says I am not in the same league as his Granny in such matters!

TARTE AUX PRUNEAUX

This is an easy version of a French classic, light years from school days prunes and custard!

12 oz/350 g ready-to-eat prunes
1 glass red wine
3 tbsp redcurrant jelly

Pastry
6 oz/175 g light plain flour
4 oz/115 g butter
1½ oz/45 g ground almonds
1½ oz/45 g caster sugar
1 egg yolk
1-2 tbsp water

Custard cream
1 rounded tbsp custard powder
5 fl oz/150 ml milk

5 fl oz/150 ml double cream, lightly whipped
sugar to taste

Almond filling
2 oz/60 g ground almonds
1½ tbsp caster sugar
½ the egg white, beaten

Pour the wine over the prunes and leave to soak.

Put all the pastry ingredients, except the water into a food processor and blend. Add the water a little at a time until a stiff paste forms. Alternatively, make as for shortcrust pastry adding the egg yolk and water after rubbing in the butter. Chill the pastry for 30 minutes, then line a 7-8 inch flan tin and bake blind, gas mark 5/190°C/375°F.

Simmer the prunes in the wine until tender, taking care that they do not boil dry. Reserve the liquid and cool the prunes. Mix the jelly with the liquid and stir until blended, set aside to cool.

Split the prunes and remove the stones and replace with the almond filling made by mixing together the ingredients.

Put the custard powder in a small pan and blend in the milk. Bring to the boil and stir until smooth. Cover and cool the fold in the whipped cream. Sweeten if necessary.

Spread the custard cream on to the pastry base. Arrange the stuffed prunes on top. Glaze with the redcurrant glaze and chill until ready to serve.

Lemon givrés (see page 33)

Summer

I am most definitely a summer person. My birthday is right in the middle of summer and I love warmth and sunshine.

There is nothing to beat eating out of doors, whether it is breakfast in the garden, tea on the lawn, a summer's evening barbecue or a picnic on the beach.

Summer brings, too, an abundance of fresh fruit, salads and vegetables, so eating can be easy and healthy, and the magical tastes can be captured in jams, jellies and preserves.

Best of all, summer means that we can escape to our little house in Provence where I can smell the herbs and the lavender, and taste the olive oil and garlic, and the other intense flavours of the south.

These days many of the ingredients are available from good shops and it is well worth trying some of the traditional recipes of the sun.

Grilled whole fish (see page 47)

VEGETABLE TERRINE WITH TOMATO SAUCE

Serves 6

4 small courgettes
2 red peppers
1 medium aubergine
6 spring onions
4 sprigs of fresh basil
2 cloves garlic
olive oil
6 eggs
salt and pepper

Tomato sauce
2 tins chopped tomatoes
1 tbsp olive oil
2 cloves garlic
1 bouquet garni (bay leaf, parsley, celery and thyme)
1 pinch sugar
salt and pepper

Preheat the oven to Gas mark 4/180°C/350°F.
Oil a 2 lb loaf tin (26 cm long)
Wash and cube all the vegetables without peeling them but making sure you remove the white pith and the seeds from the peppers.
Heat 2 tbsp oil in a frying pan. Cook the onions and courgettes for two or three minutes. Season, cover and allow to cook for a further 10 minutes. Remove the cover and allow to cook until all the liquid has evaporated.
Cook the aubergines in 4 tbsp hot oil until golden. Season and drain on kitchen paper. Blanch the peppers in boiling water, refresh in cold water then cook in oil for 5 mins.
Allow all the vegetables to cool.
Break the eggs into a bowl and beat well. Season then add the cooled vegetables, the garlic (crushed) and the basil (coarsely chopped).
Pour into the prepared tin, cover with foil and prick with a fork. Cook in the pre-heated oven for 45 minutes.
Meanwhile, prepare the tomato sauce.

Cook the tomatoes for 20 mins in a pan with the oil, bouquet garni the crushed garlic and the sugar.

Remove the bouquet and liquidise the tomatoes until smooth. Allow to cool. Chill the terrine then turn out and serve in slices accompanied by the cold sauce.

LEMON GIVRÉS

8 lemons
1 lb/500 g granulated sugar
1 pint/550 ml water
whites of 2 eggs

Finely grate the zest of two of the lemons

Cut a lid off the top of the remaining lemons, and using a lemon squeezer, squeeze the juice from each, keeping the skin intact. Reserve the skins and the lemon lids, checking that they are free of white pith and membranes.

In a heavy pan dissolve the sugar in the water, add the lemon zest, then bring to the boil. Boil for five minutes, then allow to cool completely. Add the lemon juice and pour into a plastic container. Freeze until slushy then remove and add the stiffly beaten egg white, folding it in thoroughly. Return to the freezer until firm then fill each lemon skin, heaping up the sorbet before topping with the lemon 'lid'. Store in the freezer until about 10 minutes before you serve them, balanced in pretty glasses with some Barmouth biscuits. You will probably have some lemon sorbet left for another day.

Picnics

There is a world of difference between a picnic and a packed lunch. The latter is a necessity; the former should be a pleasure and demands a modicum of planning. Ideally a *real* picnic should be piled into the car and decanted in a quiet, beautiful and reasonably accessible spot. All these are perfectly possible in the North East; what is less reliable is the weather!

Because of the unreliability of our climate it is wise to choose picnic food which is reasonably easy to manage in a confined space, i.e. the back of the car, and interesting enough to transform a forced stay at home into an occasion should this prove necessary.

Sandwiches, therefore, are out. Try instead a home-made paté with a simple salad and some crusty bread, or take a leaf out of our West Country cousins' book and go for the complete meal in one 'package'. Whatever you choose, a good sticky gingerbread goes well with a crisp apple and some Wensleydale cheese, and it's just as good in a packed lunch.

CORNISH PASTY

Makes 8 large pasties

1 lb/500 g plain flour
½ tsp salt
10 oz/300 g lard, well chilled, or use white Flora if you prefer
iced water to mix

Filling
4 oz/120 g turnip or swede, finely cubed
12 oz/350 g potatoes, finely cubed
1 large onion, chopped
1 lb/500 g lean beef topside is best, finely cubed
salt and pepper
1 egg, beaten.

First make the pastry by rubbing the fat into the flour until it resembles breadcrumbs. Or, if you are lazy like me, whizz it in the food processor. Add the iced water a little at a time until you have a firm dough. Wrap the pastry in some foil and chill for at least an hour.

Preheat the oven to gas mark 6/200°C/400°F. Grease a large baking sheet.
Roll out the pastry to about a quarter of an inch thick and cut 9 inch rounds
using a cake tin as a guide. Gather up the scraps of pastry and re-roll until you
have 8 rounds of pastry.
Toss the meat and vegetables together and season well. Place equal amounts of
mixture across the centre of each round of pastry and moisten the edge of the
circle with cold water. Bring the two halves of the circle over the filling and
seal the pastry together, then crimp the edge using thumb and two fingers.
Place on the baking sheet and brush with the beaten egg.
Cook in the preheated oven for 15 minutes, then reduce the heat to gas mark
4/150°C/350°F and continue cooking until the pastry is golden brown, about
30 minutes.

COUNTRY PATÉ

1 lb/500 g lean minced beef
1 lb/500 g belly pork, best if it is quite fat, minced
½ lb/250 g pig's liver minced
1 tbsp brandy or sherry
2 cloves of garlic crushed
1 large wine glass dry white wine or cider
6 peppercorns
6 juniper berries, not essential, but they do add an extra something
6 oz/175 g streaky bacon, unsmoked.
1 level tsp salt
A 2 lb/1 kg loaf tin or terrine.

Place the meats in a bowl and mix well together. Add half the bacon, chopped
roughly, reserve the rest in rashers to decorate the top.
Add the salt and garlic and crush the peppercorns and juniper berries before
adding them too.
Pour on the wine or cider and the brandy or sherry and give another good mix.
Cover the bowl well and leave in a cool place or in the fridge for at least a
couple of hours, longer if you can.
When you are ready to cook the paté, preheat your oven to gas mark
2/120°C/300°F. Have ready a roasting tin about a third filled with boiling

water. Pack the meat mixture into your tin or terrine, arrange the reserved bacon rashers on top and cover well. Put the tin in the roasting tin and cook in the preheated oven for about 1½ hours.

When cooked the meat will have shrunk quite a lot and there will be a delicious liquid around it. Do not drain this off because it will keep the paté moist.

Allow the paté to cool, then place a strip of foil on top and press gently. I use two tins of beans or something similar, laid on their sides. This pressing means that the paté will crumble less when cut, but it is not absolutely essential.

Some sweet pickled gherkins go very well with this, and any other coarse paté.

WEST INDIAN POTATO SALAD

1 lb/500 g new potatoes, scraped and cooked
2 or 3 chopped spring onions
1 tbsp chopped green pepper
1 stick celery, chopped
1 tbsp parsley, chopped
1 cup mayonnaise (bought, or better, homemade)
a good dash Tabasco sauce
salt and pepper

Cut the potatoes into rounds. Mix well with the rest of the ingredients and chill well.

STICKY GINGERBREAD

6 oz/175 g plain flour
2 tsp baking powder
1 tsp ground ginger
½ tsp mixed spice
pinch salt
2 oz/60 g butter
2 oz/60 g brown sugar

2 good tbsp black treacle
2 eggs
7½ fl oz/200 ml warm milk
1 tsp bicarbonate of soda

Sift together the flour, baking powder, spices and salt.
Cream the butter with the sugar and treacle and beat well.
Stir in the flour mixture and the well beaten eggs and lastly the milk with the bicarbonate of soda dissolved in it.
Beat hard until the batter is bubbly. Pour into a well greased 2 lb/1 kg loaf tin and bake in a moderate oven gas mark 3/170°C/325°F for about 40 minutes.
Cool and keep in a tin for a couple of days.

Tea on the Lawn

Although I have something of a problem because I hate tea as a beverage, I find tea, the meal, an ingenious solution to a number of entertaining problems. Visitors from abroad, who are not personal friends but who need to be entertained with a bit of style, or older friends or relatives who find a large family meal a little daunting are but two examples of ideal afternoon tea guests. If the whole event can take place in a perfect English garden on a perfect June day then so much the better. When all the elements are correct it would be difficult to think of anything more appealing.
It goes without saying that the very best china and, if available, Grandma's silver tea pot are vital to the setting. The meal should begin with wafer-thin cucumber sandwiches. To achieve very thin slices of bread you have to butter the loaf before you cut each slice.
To follow there must be scones, warm from the oven with homemade, or very good quality, jam and thick cream. If you are, like my husband, a West Countryman then the cream has to be clotted. After that it really is up to you.

BANANA BREAD

2 oz/60 g butter or margarine
4 oz/120 g caster sugar
1 egg
2 large bananas – ripe and mashed to a pulp
8 oz/240 g wholemeal self-raising flour
a little salt
3 tablespoons natural yoghurt

Cream butter and sugar together until fluffy. Beat in the egg, then the banana. Add the flour and yoghurt, alternately. Turn into a lined or well-greased 2 lb loaf tin, and bake for about an hour at gas mark 4/180°C/350°F.
This is nice on its own, or spread with butter and honey.

The centre piece has to be a cake. I decided to include my favourite; not strictly speaking traditional, because it is Australian in origin, but it is my idea of utter bliss; and it keeps in a tin for two weeks without frosting.

PASSION CAKE

6 fl oz/175 ml corn oil
6 oz/150 g caster sugar
3 eggs
1 tsp vanilla flavouring
8 oz/200 g carrots
4 oz/100 g walnut pieces, chopped
6 oz/150 g plain flour
1 tsp bicarbonate of soda
1 tsp baking powder
1 tsp cinnamon
1 tsp salt

Frosting

3 oz/75 g full-fat (cream) cheese
2 oz/50 g butter
½ tsp vanilla flavouring
4 oz/100 g icing sugar
12 walnut halves

Preheat oven to gas mark 4/180°C/350°F. Grease and line an 8½ in (22 cm) round cake tin.

Place corn oil, sugar, eggs and vanilla flavouring in a bowl; beat well.

Grate carrots, add to corn oil mixture with walnuts, flour, bicarbonate of soda, baking powder, cinnamon and salt. Mix well. Or place all ingredients except walnuts in a food processor or liquidiser, mix until the carrot is chopped, then add the walnuts.

Pour mixture into prepared tin. Bake in centre of oven for 1 hour 15 min. until cake is firm to the touch. Leave to cool in tin for 5 min. Turn out, remove paper and leave to cool completely on a wire rack.

Make frosting: place cream cheese, butter and vanilla flavouring in a bowl. Sift icing sugar in; beat till smooth. Spread over top and sides of cake. Chop 3 walnut halves and place in centre; arrange remainder around top edge.

LAZY DAISY CAKE

This recipe is one of my mum-in-law's. She thinks it was originally American and in the family it is known as 'Nutty Slack'.

2 large eggs
8 oz/250 g caster sugar
4 oz/125 g plain flour
1 tsp baking powder
few drops of vanilla essence
2 oz/50 g butter
pinch salt
4 fl oz/125 ml milk

Topping
3 tbsp melted butter
3 tbsp demerara sugar
2 tbsp cream
½ cup toasted skinned hazelnuts, crushed finely

Grease and line an 8 inch/20 cm square tin. Pre-heat oven to gas mark 5/190°C/375°F.

Whisk the eggs and vanilla, then whisk in the sugar and continue whisking until the mixture is thick and pale coloured.

Meanwhile, gently melt the butter in the milk.

Sift the flour baking powder and salt and fold into the egg mixture. Blend in the milk and butter.

Pour into the prepared tin and bake in the pre-heated oven for about 25 mins, or until springy to the touch.

Turn out on to a wire rack. Mix the topping ingredients and spread on to the top of the cake. Place under a hot grill until the top is caramelised, but watch carefully to prevent it from burning.

Cream cakes have to feature somewhere, and are easier to handle if small.

MINI CHOCOLATE ECLAIRS

Choux pastry
5 fl oz/150 ml water
2 oz/60 g butter
2½ oz/75 g plain flour
2 eggs

Set oven to gas mark 6/200°C/400°F.

Heat together water and butter in a medium pan until they bubble. Tip in the flour, and off the heat, beat well until a thick paste is formed. Cool for 5 minutes, then beat in the eggs one at a time until the mixture is smooth and glossy.

Pipe on to a damp baking-sheet using a plain nozzle in three-inch lengths.
Bake in the preheated oven for 10 minutes, then raise the temperature to gas

mark 7/220°C/425°F and continue to cook for another 10-15 minutes until crisp and brown.

Prick to release steam, and cool on a rack. Split and fill with whipped cream and top with chocolate glacé icing, not that awful chocolate 'cake covering' which has nothing at all to do with chocolate.

Self-Catering Holidays

All the time our children were young we rented and borrowed houses in this country and abroad for holidays. The children learnt a lot, had fun and we had the freedom to do as we pleased. For many people, camping, caravanning or a rented house is the ideal form of holiday, but the thought of the cooking can seem daunting.

There are three ways to approach eating on a self-catering holiday. The first is to use some of the money you save on accommodation to eat out most of the time. If you are not a keen cook then this is probably the answer, but then you wouldn't be buying a cookery book, would you?

The second approach is to pack the entire contents of your local supermarket into the car and pretend you are still at home, so why bother going?

The final way is to enjoy it. Take an interest in the local shops and markets and indulge in some creative shopping. Use the space in the car for a few essential kitchen items, a sharp knife, a heavy frying pan and, best of all, a pressure cooker, and cook simple meals from local ingredients, which will be cheaper and fresher than any other sort.

The following three recipes are good served in or out doors and need only a green salad, some scrubbed and boiled potatoes or crusty bread to make a substantial meal.

HERBED CHICKEN WITH AIOLI

1 roasting chicken
chicken stock (use a cube dissolved in a pint of water)
white wine or cider
handful of chopped fresh herbs (parsley with, for example rosemary, thyme and
basil.)
a few sliced mushrooms
2 cloves of garlic
salt and pepper.

Aioli
8 cloves garlic
3 egg yolks
olive oil
salt

You do not have to serve the aioli with the chicken. It is very good on its own but I have included the recipe to give a true Mediterranean flavour.
Loosen the skin from the chicken by pinching the breast all over, then sliding your hand between the skin and the flesh; you will feel very foolish doing this!
Scatter the herbs on the mushrooms and place on the chicken breast, under the skin.
Place the garlic in the body cavity and season.
Truss (tie up neatly) and poach the chicken in a mixture of stock and wine until tender. Serve hot or cold reserving the cooking liquid to make either a simple creamy sauce or some soup.

Aioli
Using a wooden spoon in a bowl, unless you happen to have packed your pestle and mortar, crush the garlic with the salt and mix with the egg yolks until you have a fairly smooth paste.
Add the olive oil drop by drop until you have a thick, shining golden mixture.

CHICKEN WITH FORTY CLOVES OF GARLIC

1 large roasting chicken
40 large cloves of garlic, unpeeled
fresh herbs, 2 bay leaves
salt and pepper
olive oil
a small French loaf, sliced

Season the chicken inside and stuff with a handful of fresh herbs. I like parsley, thyme and tarragon, and the bay leaves.

Place in a large casserole and surround with the unpeeled garlic cloves. Season the outside and drizzle on some olive oil.

Cover tightly and cook in a moderate oven for 1½ hours. At the end of this time remove the lid and continue cooking until golden brown, basting if necessary.

In the mean time toast the sliced French loaf or brown in the oven, brushing each slice with a little oil.

Lift the chicken on to a serving dish and keep warm while you press the cooked garlic out of each clove using the back of a knife. Spread the resulting paste on to the toasted bread and serve surrounding the chicken. I promise that the chicken will be deliciously tender and fragrant but you will not detect the garlic unless you have a slice of the bread, and even then you will be amazed by the sweetness and gentle flavour. Go on, try it!

PIPERADE

This is my own version of a Basque dish and is made in a large frying pan.

8 eggs
1 large green pepper (sliced)
1 large red pepper (sliced)
1 large onion (sliced)
½ lb/250 g ripe tomatoes (thickly sliced)
a few mushrooms
salt and pepper
3-4 oz/100 g grated cheese
finely chopped parsley
olive oil (or other oil if preferred)

In a large frying pan, cook the onion until soft. Add peppers and continue cooking until nearly done. Add mushrooms and tomatoes and cook for a few more minutes.

Meanwhile beat the eggs thoroughly and season well. Pour the eggs into the pan and stir until almost set. Add cheese and allow to melt, or pop under the grill for a few seconds. Sprinkle with parsley and serve cut in wedges with crusty bread and a green salad.

HAM, ORANGE AND CELERY RISOTTO

6 oz/175 g risotto or long grain rice
4 sticks celery, finely chopped
2 onions, finely chopped
1 green pepper, chopped
1 orange
8 oz/250 g cooked ham, diced
1 pint or a little more/600 ml hot water with a stock cube dissolved in it.
2 oz/60 g salted peanuts
seasoning

Heat the butter or oil in a frying pan and cook the vegetables gently until soft. Peel the orange and chop some of the peel finely, or grate if you are able to. Cut the orange flesh into cubes.

Add the rice to the vegetables and stir until coated with oil. Add the stock a little at a time, stirring until the rice is cooked. It is difficult to say how much stock you will need, but a good risotto has a creamy consistency and is quite moist.

Add the orange peel and the ham and heat through. Check the seasoning, then garnish with the peanuts, and some chopped parsley if available.

SALAD NIÇOISE

1 tin tuna in brine, drained and flaked
1 head lettuce, trimmed and washed
2 tomatoes
quarter of a cucumber, cut in wedges
4 hard boiled eggs
2 tbsp cooked French beans
4 cooked potatoes, cubed
8 anchovy fillets, drained
8 black olives, optional
chopped parsley
vinaigrette dressing

Tear the washed lettuce into manageable pieces and divide between 4 individual bowls.
Arrange the tomato, cucumber, beans and potatoes on the lettuce.
Put the tuna on top, arrange the egg quarters around it and decorate with the anchovies and the olives.
Dress with the vinaigrette and season well, sprinkle with the parsley and serve with crusty bread.

Barbecues

The really good thing about a barbecue is that, faced with the glowing embers, even those who usually require a grid reference to find the stove instantly turn into MasterChef.
Barbecues are cheap and universally available, even my local garage sells bags of charcoal, which is just as well because I always forget the one essential item, apart from the food.

It is quite possible to provide a banquet on a barbecue from first course to dessert. Forget the steaks and those awful 'barbecue packs' which lurk in the butchers' from early summer. They are, by and large inferior quality and lurid in colour. The rule of thumb is, if it is too tough to fry then it is much too tough to barbecue.
Don't forget the value of fish for delicious, quickly prepared barbecue meals and, most of all, don't waste the embers of the fire. Instead use them for a pudding which will really wow your family and friends.

SWEET CORN WITH HERB AND MUSTARD BUTTER

8 corn cobs (serves 8)

Herb and mustard butter
8 oz/250 g butter
1 tsp Dijon mustard
2 tbsp chopped parsley, chives and spring onions
2 tbsp lemon juice
salt and pepper

Combine the ingredients for the butter, beating well, cover and chill.
Peel back the husks of the corn but do not remove. Remove the silk. Soak the cobs in water.
Spread each cob with a tablespoon of the butter, wrap the husks back over the corn and then wrap each cob in foil.
Roast on the glowing coals for about 10-15 minutes or until tender. Remove the foil and the husks and serve with the remaining butter.

GINGER PRAWNS

3 or 4 large uncooked prawns, fresh or frozen and thawed per person

Marinade (for 8 people)
4 fl oz/120 ml sunflower oil or olive oil
3 tbsp lemon juice
1 medium onion, peeled and chopped
6 cloves garlic, crushed
1 cube (1 in/2.5 cm) fresh ginger, peeled and chopped
2 hot fresh chilli peppers, chopped
salt and pepper

Peel the prawns leaving on the tips of the tails.
Slit the back and remove the black 'string'.
Thread the prawns onto wooden skewers or satay sticks.
To two tablespoons of the oil add the lemon juice, onion, garlic and ginger, chillies, salt and pepper. Purée to a smooth paste in a blender or food processor. Marinate the prawns in this mixture for at least an hour.
Cook on a hot barbecue, brushing with the remaining oil, for about 5 minutes

only. Do not over-cook or the prawns will turn woolly in texture.
Serve with lemon wedges and a sprig of fresh herbs.

GRILLED TUNA WITH LEMON AND OLIVE OIL

4 fresh tuna steaks
2 tbsp olive oil
Juice of half a lemon
salt and pepper

Sprinkle the tuna steaks with salt and pepper and the lemon juice. Set aside for at least an hour. Heat the grill or barbecue and brush the tuna with the olive oil.
Grill for five minutes on each side. If you are cooking the fish on a cooker grill rather than a barbecue, heat a skewer in a flame and mark a criss-cross design on the steaks.
These simple and delicious steaks should be served with a simple but quite strongly flavoured accompaniment. Ratatouille, or a grilled mixed pepper salad would be perfect.
Olive oil for grilling should be of very good quality, look for extra virgin oil which is green in colour and rich in flavour.

GRILLED WHOLE FISH

1 large fish, cleaned and scaled. (or 1 small fish per person)
2 tbsp lemon juice
4 tbsp oil
bunch of fresh herbs
salt and pepper

Make some diagonal slits in the flesh of the fish. Mix the seasoning with the lemon juice and rub all over the fish, inside and out. Sprinkle with oil and then stuff the inside with the herbs.
Grill on each side until cooked. The flesh should feel firm to the touch, but still give a little.

TWO BARBECUE SWEETS

Tropical Bananas

For each serving you need:
1 ripe banana, peeled
1 tsp butter
t dsp soft brown sugar
1 tbsp rum or orange juice
2 tsp shredded coconut (optional if you hate the stuff like I do)

Place each banana on a large piece of foil.
Add the rest of the ingredients and make a package, sealing well.
Place on the grill for ten minutes and let everyone unwrap their own – the aroma is delicious.

Fresh Fruit Kebabs

Any firm fleshed fruit can be used.

Cube the fruit and thread the cubes on to skewers.
Drizzle with runny honey and a little rum or liqueur if you wish and cook on the barbecue until caramelised.

Croquembouche (see page 63)

Autumn

I have very mixed feelings when the leaves begin to change colour and the days grow shorter. The end of summer is sad and the excitement of the Christmas season seems a long way off. There are however, compensations in the kitchen. Devoted preservers are in their element making jams, pickles and chutneys and there are all sorts of reasons to have a family celebration. Autumn seems to be a good time to bake bread and scones, particularly if you have homemade jam to spread on them, and clever cooks will start to make edible gifts for Christmas giving; presented in attractive containers, they will save time and money in the mad Christmas rush.

Bramble mousse (see page 54)
Mushroom soup (see page 52)

Food for Free

It must be my Scots blood, but I absolutely love getting something for nothing. Autumn means free food everywhere for the picking. I must have been a country dweller in a former life because I make stones of preserves every year and give most away. I simply have to turn fruits, berries and mushrooms into something good to eat. It is a great shame that we neglect so many good things in this country. Take wild mushrooms for instance; they cost a fortune in France and yet grow in profusion in this country. Perhaps if we, like the French, could take samples of mushrooms to our local chemist for identification and advice we might be more inclined to use them.

MUSHROOM SOUP

8 oz/250 g mushrooms, wiped and chopped finely
1 onion
1 tbsp butter or oil
1½ tbsp plain flour
15 fl oz/450 ml water or stock
15 fl oz/450 ml milk
chopped parsley and a little cream to garnish

In a large pan melt the butter and cook the onion until soft but not coloured. Add the mushrooms and cook for a further 2 or 3 minutes.
Stir in the flour and continue to cook for a few minutes before adding the milk and water or stock. Bring to the boil and cook for about 5 minutes. Season well and serve with a sprinkling of parsley and a swirl of cream. Simple and absolutely delicious.

MUSHROOM CORNUCOPIA

8 oz/250 g puff pastry
3 tbsp olive oil
1 clove garlic (crushed)
2 shallots, finely chopped

18 oz/500 g assorted wild mushrooms, fresh (or dried and soaked)
7 oz/200 g fresh tomato slices
2 tbsp chopped fresh herbs
salt, pepper and paprika

Prepare pastry cones using strips of rolled out puff pastry wrapped around cream horn moulds, glazed and baked.

While these are cooking, sweat the garlic and shallots in the olive oil for a couple of minutes.

Stir in the sliced mushrooms, adding the firmest ones first and the softer ones later. Sauté over a high heat until the mushrooms begin to be tender.

Add the rest of the ingredients, using the paprika to taste.

When warmed through fill the pastry horns and serve immediately.

Blackberries are one of my favourite fruits. I love them in pies and crumbles when combined with apples or, more usually with pears. A straightforward crumble topping made with wholemeal flour and brown sugar is particularly delicious with this combination.

A word of warning: if you are going blackberrying, choose a spot away from main roads. Apart from the obvious traffic hazards, plants absorb lead from car exhausts. Even in these days of lead-free petrol I would not fancy some of the fruit I see being collected.

If you collect enough to freeze, and they do freeze well, it is better to freeze them unwashed and wash them before use. Grubs and bugs will then float away.

When you get sick of bramble pies and crumbles, the following recipe is light, full of flavour and very easy. A tip for using gelatine: always add gelatine to water, not the other way round, and dissolve over hot water or at a very low setting for 2 minutes in the microwave. If you overheat gelatine it forms nasty strings.

BRAMBLE MOUSSE

1 lb/450 g blackberries, washed
4 oz/100 g caster sugar
1 tbsp gelatine powder
2 tbsp water
1 tbsp lemon juice
5 fl oz/140 ml double cream
2 egg whites

Put the blackberries in a pan but keep a few back for decoration.
Cook until they are soft and the juices are running.
Sprinkle the gelatine on the water. Dissolve the gelatine over hot water or in a microwave. Stir the lemon juice into the gelatine.
Rub the blackberries through a nylon sieve. Stir in the gelatine mixture and leave to cool.
Whip the cream and when the blackberry mixture begins to set, fold the cream into it. Beat the egg whites until stiff and fold into the mixture.
Spoon into a serving dish, or into individual glasses. Chill until set. Decorate with whole berries and more whipped cream if you like.

Elderberries are another plentiful free food. The same rule about picking from trees on main roads apply. Combined with apple they make a rich, dark jelly which is good on toast or muffins, but also with rich meats like pork or venison as an addition to the gravy or as an accompaniment.

ELDERBERRY JELLY

2 lbs/1 kg apples or crab apples chopped but not peeled
2 lbs/1 kg ripe elderberries
about 3 cups sugar
2 tbsp lemon juice

Place the fruit in a large pan and cover with water. Bring to the boil and simmer for 25/30 mins, or until the fruit is very tender.

Tip the contents of the pan into a jelly bag over a large bowl and let it drain for several hours.

Measure the juice and for every 2 cups add 1 of sugar. Place in a pan, add the lemon juice and cook the mixture over a low heat until the sugar has melted. Boil, skimming it if necessary until the jelling point is reached. To test this, drop a small amount on to a cold plate, leave for a short time then push with your finger. If the jelly wrinkles, then it is ready.

Pot in dry sterilised jars and seal.

Hallowe'en

Hallowe'en is an excellent excuse for a party and one which can be enjoyed by the whole family. If you ignore the annoying and positively dangerous 'Trick or Treat' and go for another American tradition in the shape of a pumpkin you can provide both ingredient and decor in one recipe. It is fun to share such celebrations with the whole age range, which can pose some menu problems. These can be simply overcome if you stick to familiar ingredients and give them an original twist.

PUMPKIN SOUP

1 pumpkin (4-5 lbs/2 kg in weight)
1 tin chopped tomatoes
2 medium onions
3 medium sized potatoes
2 tbsp uncooked rice
seasoning
small carton double cream to finish (optional)

Cut a lid off the top of the pumpkin and hollow out the inside. First remove the seeds. These can be washed, lightly fried, drained and sprinkled with salt for nibbles.

Hollow out the flesh using a metal spoon. Be careful not to puncture the skin. Cut the pumpkin flesh into small pieces.

In a little oil or butter, soften the onion, then add the potato, the pumpkin and the tin of tomatoes. Add 3 pints/1.5 litres of water, season and bring to the boil. Simmer for 20-30 mins. or until the vegetables are cooked.

Sieve or liquidise and return to the pan. If the soup seems too thick, and this depends on the texture of the pumpkin, add a little milk or stock. Check the seasoning and add half the cream if you are using it. Set the pumpkin on a plate and pour the soup into the shell. With the rest of the cream make 3 or 4 circles on top of the soup, simply by pouring it in a steady stream. Then take a pointed knife and draw lines from the centre through the cream to make a spider's web effect. This sounds more complicated than it is!

For a main course I suggest something which can be eaten with the fingers, though you will need plenty of paper napkins! To accompany the spare ribs, jacket potatoes with fromage frais and chives and a mixed salad, or matchsticks of raw vegetables should please young and old alike.

BARBECUED SPARE RIBS

Serves 8

5 lbs/2 kg spare ribs. Not spare rib chops but the ribs of pork from the top of the neck.

Sauce
2 tsp salt
4 tbsp soy sauce
2 tbsp soft brown sugar
6 tbsp tomato ketchup
4 tbsp runny honey
1 tsp chilli and garlic sauce
2 cups stock, made with a cube if you like

Mix the sauce ingredients together and marinate the ribs in it for at least an hour.

Set the oven to gas mark 5/190°C/375°F.

Lift the ribs out of the marinade and reserve it. Place the ribs on a rack in a roasting tin. Add a little water to prevent smoking and roast in the heated oven for about 1½ hours, turning the ribs quite frequently.
Meanwhile boil up the marinade, adding a little extra stock if desired.
When the ribs are cooked, place them on a serving dish and pour the sauce over them.

DEVILLED DRUMSTICKS

Serves 8

16 small chicken drumsticks
2 onions
2 carrots, peeled and sliced
bouquet garni
½ tsp black peppercorns
salt

Devil mixture
4 oz/125 g butter
2 tbsp tomato sauce
2 tbsp Worcestershire sauce
1 tsp ground mace
2 tbsp fruity chutney, homemade if possible, but otherwise, mango
salt and pepper
anchovy essence
Tabasco sauce
watercress to garnish

Put the chicken into a large pan with the vegetables, bouquet garni and peppercorns. Barely cover with water, cover with a lid and simmer for 15 minutes. Allow the chicken to cool slightly in the liquid.
Prepare the devil mixture by creaming the butter thoroughly then gradually mixing in the other ingredients.
Take out the chicken pieces and drain, then remove the skin. Spread a little devil mixture on each.

Cook on a pre-heated grill until well browned adding the remaining devil mixture during cooking. These can be served hot or cold, garnished with watercress.

Any dessert for an autumn party should include ingredients which are seasonal. For pudding therefore, I suggest something which any age group will enjoy.

UPSIDE DOWN PEAR AND CHOCOLATE PUDDING

Base
1 tin, or 3 fresh pears; if fresh, peeled, halved and poached until tender
2 oz/60 g butter
2 tbsp dark brown soft sugar
Cherries and walnuts or pecan nuts to decorate

Cake
4 oz/125 g self raising flour
4 oz/125 g caster sugar
4 oz/125 g butter or margarine
1 tbsp cocoa powder
2 eggs

In a 7 or 8 inch (20 cm) round cake tin melt the butter and sugar for the base. Arrange the pear halves with the nuts and cherries as desired.

Cream the fat and sugar for the cake until pale and fluffy. Add the eggs, one at a time, beating between each addition.

Sieve the flour and cocoa powder and add to the mixture. Fold in with a metal spoon.

Spoon over the pears and bake in a medium oven gas mark 5/190°C/375°F until the cake is firm to the touch. Invert on to a serving plate and serve warm or hot with thick cream or yoghurt.

Bonfire Night

An evening for kids of all ages, and the same suggestions apply as for Hallowe'en. It matters little if you are going to an organised display or lighting the blue touch paper in the back garden. After it is all over you will be faced with cold, hungry people and over-excited kids so fancy food is out. Bangers are the obvious theme, but so many sausages bought from supermarkets are of poor quality that it really is worth making your own.

Fresh sausages are easy enough to make and do not require skins. You will have the added satisfaction of knowing exactly what went into them and you can also reduce the amount of fat if this is important, although if you do it is wise to add a little beaten egg to bind them together.

HOMEMADE PORK SAUSAGES

5 oz/150 g bread, this should not be too new and can be white or wholemeal
1/2 pint/300 ml water
1 lb/450 g lean pork
5 oz/150 g firm pork fat
1/2 tsp ground mace
1 tsp salt
good pinch dried sage and ground ginger
a little flour for shaping

Remove the crust from the bread and cut it into cubes. Soak in the water in a bowl.
Cut up the pork and the fat roughly and combine with the seasoning. Squeeze the water from the bread and add to the meat. Work in a food processor, you may have to do this a bit at a time.
Shape into sausages on a floured surface. You will make about 14 plump sausages. Chill.
Shallow fry or grill. These sausages may be frozen before cooking.

The next recipe is perfect for Bonfire night. It will stay happily in a low oven until you are ready to eat it or it can be reheated without harm. It comes from my own hard-up student days when I had invited friends for supper, but only had enough money for some sausages to go with the things already in the cupboard. It is still a family favourite.

SAUSAGE AND BEAN CASSEROLE

1 lb/450 g good quality sausages, homemade or bought
1 large tin baked beans
3 or 4 large potatoes, peeled and thinly sliced
1 onion, thinly sliced
1 tsp mixed dried herbs
salt and pepper
dash Worcestershire sauce
1 cup stock

If the sausages are large, twist them in the middle and cut each in half.
In a large casserole layer the ingredients starting with the beans and seasoning each layer.
Finish with a layer of potatoes and cook in a moderate oven for 1½ hours or until the potatoes are soft. Remove lid and crisp the potatoes for the last 15 minutes.

SAUSAGE, BEAN AND BACON SOUP

1 oz/25 g butter or margarine
1 large onion, chopped
1 celery stick, sliced
1 carrot, sliced
1 clove garlic, crushed
4 oz/125 g bacon, chopped
4 oz/125 g sliced spicy sausage (chorizo or kabanos)
1 tbsp flour
2 pints/1.25 l hot vegetable stock, Oxo vegetable cubes are good
2 tsp Worcestershire sauce

a good pinch mixed dried herbs
1 can red kidney beans, drained and rinsed
1 large can baked beans

Melt butter in a large pan and cook the onion, celery and carrot until soft. Add garlic and bacon and cook until soft. Stir in the flour and cook for a minute. Gradually add the stock, Worcestershire sauce, herbs and seasoning and stir until boiling. Cover and simmer gently for 20 minutes.
Stir in the beans and sausage and cook gently for a further five minutes or until heated through.
This soup freezes well.

STUFFED SAUSAGES

Per person

3 chipolata sausages or 2 larger sausages, grilled and well drained on kitchen paper.

Split lengthways and fill with one of the following:
1 low fat cheese slice, a tsp of chutney and a little cress.
Low fat cottage cheese with chopped herbs or pineapple.
Sage and onion or other left-over stuffing.

Finally, an alternative to the familiar, but often dreary sausage roll using one of the continental sausages now readily available in supermarkets. I have tried both mini Chorizos which are Spanish sausages flavoured with paprika, and Kabanos which are smoked, spicy Polish sausages. Both work well.

SPICY SAUSAGE PARCELS

Makes 20

2 packs mini chorizos or kabanos
7 sheets of fillo pastry. Use the large size, if you use Jus Rol brand you will need
more because the sheets are smaller
2 oz/60 g butter
Sesame seeds to garnish

Melt the butter and brush half of each pastry sheet with some of it. Fold the sheet over and cut into lengths about twice as long as each sausage.
Place each sausage on one double rectangle and fold in the sides then roll up the sheet and place on a buttered baking sheet. Brush with melted butter and sprinkle with sesame seeds.
When all the sausages are wrapped, bake in a moderate oven gas mark 5/190°C/375°F until they are brown and crisp. Serve hot with a grain mustard or a barbecue sauce to dip them in. If you like you can spread each sausage with a little French mustard before rolling them up.

Special Birthday Cakes

I know that you can pop into all sorts of places to buy a birthday cake all ready made, but they are expensive and if you have a very special birthday to celebrate it can be part of your gift to prepare a very special cake. This can be as simple as a madeira cake or sponge covered with 'ready to roll' icing and decorated with a personal touch. Paper cocktail umbrellas, gold covered chocolate coins, or silly lollipops tied around the edge with a bright ribbon are just a few ideas. If, however you have something more sophisticated in mind you may have to work a little harder!

A Very Special Birthday Cake
Its posh name is *Croquembouche*, literally 'crunch-in-mouth', and it is often served at weddings in France. It is essentially a pyramid of small choux pastry buns dipped in caramel and surrounded by a web of spun sugar. Although it looks spectacular it is really not hard to make with a little time and patience.

This version is one I saw recently in France and included stuffed dried fruits and nuts with marzipan sweets. I thought it made a very special end to a special meal, as everyone just breaks off whatever they fancy.

Real spun sugar is time consuming and messy to make but there is an easy way to make a similar effect. It should not be made too far ahead, however, because the caramel which holds it together will begin to melt.

Take time to read through the recipe before you begin; this is a wise move when tackling any lengthy recipe for the first time.

CROQUEMBOUCHE

For choux pastry
7½ fl oz/215 ml water
3 oz/75 g unsalted butter
3¾ oz/95 g fine plain flour
3 eggs

Set the oven to gas mark 6/200°C/400°F.

Put the water and butter into a fairly large saucepan. Sift the flour onto a piece of paper.

Bring the water and butter to the boil and as soon as it bubbles up, tip in the flour, remove the pan from the heat and stir vigorously until the mixture is smooth.

Leave to cool for five minutes or so, then beat in the eggs, one at a time. When you get to the last egg, beat it and add a little at a time so as not to have too sloppy a mixture. It should be firm and hold its shape.

Beat the mixture until smooth and glossy then place it in a piping bag fitted with a medium plain nozzle.

Dampen two large baking sheets and pipe out small blobs of choux leaving space for them to rise or form small balls using a teaspoon.

Cook in the preheated oven for ten minutes then raise the heat to gas mark 7/220°C/425°F until the buns are golden and crisp. This will take a further ten minutes or so.

Cool on a wire rack, then split and fill with whipped cream or thick custard. The buns can be made ahead of time. If so, do not fill them and refresh them in a warm oven for a few minutes if they have been kept overnight or frozen. Cool and fill as above.

To assemble
12 ready-to-eat prunes, stones removed.
12 dates, stones removed
½ lb/250 g marzipan
walnut halves and whole blanched almonds
glacé cherries
silver balls
taper candles or sparklers

Caramel
10 tbsp granulated sugar
10 tbsp water

Choose a really attractive plate on which to serve your creation.

I have some Edwardian and Victorian glass cake stands which I have collected from jumble sales and junk shops for a couple of pounds at the most. They are perfect for this sort of thing.

Stuff the dates and prunes with a small sausage of marzipan and decorate with nuts, cherry halves or silver balls.

Use the remaining marzipan to make little petits fours, topped with nuts or cherries.

Make sure you have everything to hand before starting the last part of the process.

To make the caramel, put the water and sugar in a heavy pan and warm over a gentle heat until the sugar is completely dissolved. Do not stir it or allow it to come to the boil until it has all dissolved or the caramel will go grainy. Have ready a large bowl of cold water.

Once the sugar has dissolved then increase the heat and boil steadily until the caramel is a golden colour. This will take about ten minutes.

Immediately dip the bottom of the pan into the cold water to stop the cooking. Now you must work fast so you must have everything close at hand.

Using some tongs, dip a choux bun into the caramel and place the bun on the plate. Repeat with a second bun, placing it right next to the first so that it sticks. Continue in this way to form a circle of about ten buns. Now start a second circle on top of the first, this time make the circle smaller, to form the base of the pyramid, the caramel will hold it all together and your pyramid will be hollow.

The third circle should be of the stuffed prunes, also dipped in the caramel.

Continue with two more rows of buns and then the dates. Finally top off with a small circle of buns and a final one on the top.

Place the petits fours around the base then take two forks, held together with points facing inwards. Dip these into the remaining caramel which should be quite stiff by now. Pull up the forks and you will find that the caramel comes up in spiders web strings. Wrap these fine threads around your creation and continue to dip and wrap until the sugar becomes too hard.

Add taper candles or sparklers.

Don't panic about the state of the pan. To clean it just fill with hot water and leave until the caramel dissolves.

South Seas Christmas pudding (see page 78)

Winter

If you love cooking for other people you have to enjoy the winter season, even if a bit of you is longing to be picking fresh basil in the sun. I simply can't imagine Christmas without a houseful of family and friends, and my husband suggesting we eat out next year and not meaning a word of it. Somehow this time of year epitomises the joys and trials of the person who cooks for love. It requires thought, planning and organisation, a bit of cheating and the heavy reliance upon the good nature of anyone who happens to wander into the kitchen. Gifts of food are, perhaps, the most appreciated by older folk, single people and those who are even more harassed than you. These can be made and stored throughout the year, but come the Festive Season you really do need some extra tricks up the culinary sleeve.

Gallantine of chicken with ham and pistachio nut mousse (see page 71)

Cooking for a Crowd

There are all sorts of reasons throughout the year to entertain. Whenever the number of guests exceeds the number of chairs then thoughts turn to a buffet. Food for such an event needs to be good looking, easy to eat and, most importantly be quick to prepare. The ubiquitous quiche is therefore out. Dishes need to be prepared in advance or even frozen. Don't make the common mistake of making too many different dishes; this only results in the less discriminating guests heaping their plates with a sample of everything in a confusion of conflicting tastes and textures. Make sure that whatever you serve can be eaten on a bendy paper plate with a fork without risk to the carpet, and you will be well on the way to a happy party.

CROSTINI

Enough for 8

1 long French loaf, 2 days old
olive oil
1 packet frozen chicken livers, thawed, drained and chopped
1 medium onion finely chopped
2 cloves garlic, crushed
1 cup chopped tinned tomatoes
½ tsp mixed dried herbs
a little red wine

Slice the bread quite thinly and brush with olive oil. Place on a baking sheet and brown in a moderate oven for a few minutes.
In a pan, soften the onion and garlic in a little olive oil. Add the chicken livers and cook through. Add the tomatoes, herbs, seasoning and a little wine and cook until thick, adding a little more wine to moisten if necessary. Spread on to the bread and serve hot, sprinkled with chopped parsley or chives.
If you want to be really quick then use some of the excellent ready made Italian ranges in jars. I love the *pomodori secchi* sun-dried tomatoes in olive oil.

POACHED SALMON IN PINK WINE ASPIC

Serves 20

1 7 lb/3 kg fresh salmon
fresh dill and parsley
1 bottle dry rosé wine
1 pkt aspic powder
salt and pepper
1 bunch radishes
1/2 cucumber

Get your fishmonger to clean the salmon. Fill the body cavity with fresh dill and parsley and season well.

Line a very large roasting tin with foil and curve the salmon into the tin. Pour in a couple of glasses of the wine and seal with more foil.

Bake in a moderate oven for about 10 minutes per pound or until the fish feels firm to the touch and the skin peels away easily.

Leave to cool in the cooking liquid then lift carefully out of the tin and remove the skin from the body of the fish. Remove the herbs and place the fish on a serving plate.

Make up the aspic using wine instead of the water in the directions. Leave to cool until it begins to go syrupy. Brush a coat of the aspic over the salmon and leave to set. Meanwhile, trim the radishes and cut into rounds. Cut the cucumber into thin slices and halve each slice.

Arrange the radish and cucumber slices down the backbone of the fish and around the edge, adding small sprigs of dill here and there.

Brush over another layer or two of aspic and allow the rest to run over the plate to form a pretty base.

GALLANTINE OF CHICKEN WITH HAM AND PISTACHIO NUT MOUSSE

Serves 10

1 large roasting chicken
1 1/2 lb/1 kg gammon
2 eggs
10 fl oz/300 ml double cream
2 tbsp pistachio nuts
salt and pepper

Ask your butcher to bone out the chicken for you. Most good butchers will do this if given enough notice.

In a food processor, blend the raw ham until smooth, add the eggs and blend again. Lightly whip the cream and fold into the ham and finally, fold in the nuts.

Season the inside of the chicken and fill with the mousse. Tie up the chicken into a neat parcel. Brush the outside with butter and season then wrap in foil. Weigh the chicken.

Cook in a moderate oven for 25 minutes per lb/450 g or until a skewer inserted into the meat produces clear juices.

Allow to cool wrapped in the foil and refrigerate until needed. To serve slice quite thinly and arrange on a plate.

SALMON KOULIBIAC

Each one serves 6/8 so make as many as you need

1 pkt frozen puff pastry
12 oz/375 g salmon, skinned and boned
1 medium onion
4 oz/125 g butter
4 oz/125 g uncooked long grain rice
2 eggs, hard boiled
1 tbsp chopped parsley and dill; the dill could be dried
salt and pepper and a dash of Tabasco sauce
2 tbsp fresh breadcrumbs

Begin by cooking the salmon, either wrapped in foil in the oven, or on a plate in your microwave.

Cook the rice in plenty of boiling water, then drain well.

Melt 1 oz/25 g butter in a pan and cook the finely chopped onion until soft. Add the rice with the flaked salmon, the chopped hard boiled egg and the seasoning.

Roll out the pastry into a 10 in/25 cm square and dampen the edges with water. Pile the fish and rice mixture into the centre of the pastry making a diamond shape which leaves triangles of pastry uncovered. Take each corner of the pastry and bring them to the middle, sealing the edges together with your thumb and fingers. This leaves a small hole at the centre. Place on a baking sheet and brush with melted butter and sprinkle with breadcrumbs. Cook in a hot oven gas mark 6/200°C/400°F until the pastry is risen and golden brown. Just before serving pour the rest of the melted butter through the hole in the top. If you wish to be very indulgent then serve a jug of more butter with the koulibiac.

Serve a variety of salads with this main course. I like a mixture of fresh bean sprouts, orange slices, sliced raw mushrooms and peanuts in a lemony French dressing. Halved cherry tomatoes and watercress make a colourful quick salad. If you serve a green salad, and it goes very well with koulibiac, then tear the leaves up quite small so that they can be managed with a fork. Do not add the dressing until the last minute, or the salad will go limp.

Christmas Day

Much as I love tradition, I also like to insert a hint of innovation into the celebrations. For instance, I don't always cook what is now considered to be the traditional turkey for the main Christmas meal.

Goose was, in fact, the choice of those who could afford, or rear, it long before turkey arrived from the New World. It is expensive and can, unless carefully cooked, be very rich indeed. The addition of fruit to the stuffing is a tradition from Europe which helps with the balance of the dish.

I make a very traditional pudding in October each year for the Christmas in the NEXT year. With careful storage and the judicious addition of rum the result is dark, rich and utterly delicious. I know that there are many people who find the pud a bit of a trial at the end of a heavy meal, so perhaps a lighter alternative in the same vein would be more acceptable.

One also needs to consider edible gifts, which double as additions to your own table.

FRUIT STUFFED GOOSE.

1 ready-to-eat goose weighing 7 lbs/3 kg
1 chicken stock cube
2 tbsp oil
salt and pepper

Stuffing
4 Cox's apples
7 oz/200 g ready-to-eat dried apricots
1 large carrot
7 oz/200 g walnut halves
1 lb/500g onions
7 oz/200 g smoked streaky bacon
juice of 1 lemon
1 tbsp oil
4 tbsp brandy
1/2 tsp mixed spice

First prepare the stuffing. Cut the apricots into fine strips, put them in a bowl with the brandy and leave to soak.

Peel and finely chop the onions. Peel the carrot and the apples and grate them coarsely, then sprinkle with the lemon juice.

Coarsely chop the walnuts. Dice the bacon.

Heat the oil in a large pan and cook the onions gently without allowing them to colour. Once they are transparent, add the bacon and mix in the grated carrot and apple. Season and cook gently for about 10 mins.

Heat the oven to gas mark 8/230°C/450°F.

Tip the contents of the pan into a mixing bowl and add the nuts, the apricots and brandy and the spice. Season and mix well.

Stuff the neck end of the goose and secure the flap with trussing threads or cocktail sticks.

Put the goose on a rack in a roasting tin and rub with the oil. Cook for an hour in the pre-heated oven, then pour on the stock made from the cube and 8 fl oz/250 ml boiling water.

Lower the oven temperature to gas mark 4/180°C/350°F and cook for a further hour or until the juices run clear, basting frequently with the pan juices. Use the pan juices to make a rich gravy.

The following stuffing is absolutely delicious in boned chicken or turkey. If you ask your butcher nicely he will do the boning for you. Poultry or joints done in this way are much easier to carve.

HAM AND BRAZIL NUT STUFFING

The quantity given will be enough for a 6 lb/3 kg bird

1 lb/500 g corner gammon joint
1 oz/25 g butter
1 small onion, finely chopped
4 oz/125 g white breadcrumbs
4 oz/125 g Brazil nuts, roughly chopped
1 tsp tomato purée
1 tsp finely grated orange zest
1 egg, beaten
½ tsp ground mace

Cut the gammon into small pieces and fry in the butter for 2 or 3 minutes only. Remove the ham and soften the onion in the same pan.
Put the ham and onion through a mincer, or whizz in a blender briefly. Mix in the other ingredients and bind with the egg. Use as required.

A THOUSAND WAYS WITH TURKEY

If you do decide to cook the traditional turkey, what do you do with the leftovers?

Sandwiches, you don't have to eat them now, make up a batch and put into individual bags then freeze and rescue in January or February when packed lunches look boring.

If you mince (or whizz in a blender) the turkey meat and add a little cooked ham, a little mayonnaise and some paprika the resulting sandwich spread can be used now or stored in the freezer for later.

Make a spectacular salad which is good enough for a dinner party combining cubed turkey with some chopped dried apricots, and some salted cashew nuts. Add a teaspoon of curry paste to a cup of mayonnaise and use to bind the salad together. Serve on a bed of crisp lettuce.

Use as a filling for vol-au-vents. Make a well flavoured white sauce, add some cooked bacon and a few mushrooms both chopped and cooked together, then the finely cubed turkey. Use the resulting mixture to fill vol-au-vent cases freshly cooked (but use the frozen sort!)

Thread chunky pieces of cooked turkey onto a skewer, alternating with bacon rolls, cherry tomatoes, mushrooms and squares of green pepper. Brush with oil, sprinkle with mixed herbs and grill until the bacon is crisp.

Combine chopped or minced turkey with an equal amount of mixed frozen vegetables. Make a white sauce, using a little wine mixed with the milk, season well then use to fill a flan dish lined with pastry, top with a lid, glaze and cook until golden brown.

Curry it.

Make a vegetable chilli, add diced cooked turkey and heat through thoroughly.

Remember that any reheated food should be heated right through.

Take all the meat off the carcass and store it carefully, you can even freeze some for later use. Use the smarter bits with salads and pickles, the scrappier bits minced and used as suggested. Make a big pan of stock with the carcass and turn it into soup, no-one will object to that and the body will not be there staring at you reproachfully throughout the holiday!

Use strips to top a pizza (use a packet base mix) with strips of ham and some olives on the usual tomato base.

Tell your fortune with the wish bone.

Combine finely chopped turkey with sautéed mushrooms and a little double cream and fresh parsley to make a delicious filling for omlettes or pancakes.

Make a rissotto using cubed turkey and mushrooms with some fresh herbs.

An American Chef's salad consists of very finely sliced strips of turkey or chicken, ham and cheese on a bed of lettuce, tomato, spring onions and cucumber with a Thousand Island dressing.

Make turkey burgers to serve on a toasted bun with a spoonful of chutney and sliced onion rings.

1 oz/25 g butter
medium onion peeled and chopped
1 tbsp flour
1 cup light stock (use a cube if necessary)
12 oz/350 g minced cooked turkey
2 tbsp lemon juice
2 tbsp chopped parsley
½ tsp turmeric
2 eggs
salt and pepper
fresh breadcrumbs
oil for frying

Melt the butter and add the onion. Cook until tender, stir in the flour and the stock and stir until boiling.
Add the rest of the ingredients and one of the eggs, beaten, then allow to cool. When cold, shape into 8 burgers, egg and crumb then fry in shallow oil until golden.

Buy a goose next year.

SOUTH SEAS CHRISTMAS PUDDING

Medium can of pineapple rings in juice
4 oz/125 g soft margarine
4 oz/125 g caster sugar
rind of one orange, grated
2 eggs beaten
3 oz/90 g self raising flour
2 oz/60 g fresh breadcrumbs
2 oz/60 g raisins
2 oz/60 g glacé cherries, halved
2 oz/60 g ready-to-eat dried apricots, chopped
2 tbsp golden syrup

Drain the pineapple and cut the rings into halves, reserve three halves. Chop the rest.
Cream the margarine and sugar. Add the orange rind and beat in the eggs. Fold in the flour and breadcrumbs. Add the chopped pineapple, raisins, cherries and apricots and mix well.
Butter a 1½ pint basin and put the syrup in the bottom. Arrange the reserved pineapple in a circle and spoon the mixture on top. Cover with greaseproof and then foil. Steam the pudding for one and three quarter hours and serve hot.
To freeze, leave to get cold then wrap the whole basin in foil. Label and store for up to three months. To serve, allow to thaw and re-wrap before steaming for about an hour.

MICROWAVE CHRISTMAS PUDDING

Serves 4-6
Power setting: 700 watts

3 oz/75 g fresh brown breadcrumbs
3 oz/75 g plain flour
pinch of mace
pinch of nutmeg

pinch of cinnamon
3 oz/75 g shredded beef suet
4 oz/100 g dark soft sugar
2 oz/50 g sultanas
5 oz/150 g raisins
2 oz/50 g cherries, quartered
1½ oz/40 g blanched almonds, chopped
1 small cooking apple, peeled, cored and chopped
grated rind and juice of ½ lemon
1 tbsp brandy
1 large egg, beaten
3 tbsps brown ale or stout
1 tbsp milk
1½ tbsps black treacle

In a large mixing bowl mix the breadcrumbs with the flour, mace, nutmeg, cinnamon, suet and sugar. Add the peel, currants, sultanas, raisins, almonds, apple and cherries, mixing well. Blend the lemon rind and juice with the brandy, egg, ale or stout, milk and treacle. Add to the dry ingredients, mixing to make a mixture with a soft dropping consistency – add a little extra milk if necessary. Cover the mixture and leave overnight or for 6-8 hours.
Turn into a greased 1.15 litre/2 pint pudding basin. Cover loosely with cling film and cook for 8 minutes. Leave to rest in the basin for 5 minutes before turning out and serving with custard, cream or brandy butter.
You can store this pudding for up to 2 weeks – any longer it's best to freeze it. If the pudding is cooked in advance and needs reheating, thaw if necessary and cook for 2-3 minutes, then serve.

SPICED ORANGE SLICES

12 thin-skinned oranges
2½ lbs/1 kg sugar, light brown or white, as you wish
1 pint/550 ml white wine vinegar
1 tsp whole cloves
1 large stick cinnamon
6-8 blades mace

Wash the oranges and slice very thinly, remove any pips. Put the slices in a large pan.

Cover with cold water, bring to the boil and simmer gently, covered, until the oranges are barely tender.

In another pan, bring the remaining ingredients to the boil, stirring until the sugar has dissolved. Boil for 3 mins. Remove the orange slices with a slotted spoon and add to the vinegar. Add enough of the orange cooking water to just cover the slices and simmer until they are tender and translucent. Be careful not to allow them to disintegrate. Remove the pan from the heat and leave the oranges in the syrup for twenty four hours.

Carefully remove the orange slices with a slotted spoon and place them in sterilised jars, filling the jars only half full.

Bring the syrup to the boil again and boil for a few moments to reduce a little. Allow to cool a little then fill the jars and seal. The oranges will be ready in a few weeks and are excellent with all sorts of cold meats.

SPICED OLIVES

½ lb/250 g pitted green olives in brine, I use Sainsbury's own brand, or Crespo brand
2 cloves garlic
½ pint/300 ml white wine vinegar
1 tbsp light brown sugar
thinly peeled rind of 1 orange
small piece cinnamon stick
½ tsp mixed peppercorns, crushed
8 coriander seeds, crushed

Drain the olives and put them into a jar, or jars, filling them almost to the top. Peel and slice the garlic and put it, with all the remaining ingredients, into a pan. Bring to the boil and simmer for five minutes. Allow to cool a little and pour into the jars to come to the top. Seal.

Once opened, the olives are best kept in the fridge, so label accordingly.

SHERRIED PRUNES

These make a delicious accompaniment to Christmas meats, especially pork and game. They also make a good nibble with drinks especially if you fill the centre with cream cheese.

1 pkt ready-to-eat stoned prunes
medium dry sherry to cover (impossible to give exact quantities)
1 cinnamon stick for each jar
1 strip of thinly sliced orange peel for each jar

Fill pretty glass jars with the prunes, being careful not to pack them too tightly. Slip a cinnamon stick and a piece of orange peel into each jar and top up with sherry. Seal and leave in a cool place for several weeks. It may be necessary to top up the jars with sherry as the prunes absorb the liquid.

European Christmas Cakes

All over the Christian world special cakes are made for Christmas. This does not necessarily mean a replica snow scene with plastic robins. I don't particularly care for marzipan and icing, especially rock hard royal icing, so I make something a bit different which incorporates the glacé fruit from my other home, near Apt in France. This is the self-proclaimed world capital of crystallised fruit. The produce is available at good shops in this country. The recipe, I believe, came to me years ago from 'someone in Alnwick castle' so it isn't too foreign after all. The other cakes are for those who prefer something lighter or, in the case of the French *Bûche de Noël*, without dried fruit, though not, I have to say, calories.

GLAZED FRUIT CHRISTMAS CAKE

8 oz/225 g unsalted butter
8 oz/225 g soft brown sugar
grated rind 1 lemon
5 eggs
8 oz/225 g light plain flour
1 tsp mixed spice
8 oz/225 g chopped nuts
12 oz/35o g mixed glacé fruit, chopped
1 lb/450 g sultanas and raisins
2 tsp lemon juice
To finish: 8 oz/225 g mixed glacé fruit
2 tbsp rum
2 oz/50 g demerara sugar

Preheat the oven to gas mark 4/180°C/350°F.
Grease and line an 8 inch/20 cm round cake tin.
Cream together the butter and sugar with the lemon rind. Beat in the eggs.
Sift the flour and mix with the spice, nuts, glacé and dried fruit.
Add to the creamed mixture with the lemon juice and fold in with a metal spoon.
Spoon into the prepared tin. Tie a piece of brown paper round the outside and bake in the preheated oven for about 4½ hours or until cooked through, test with a skewer.
Meanwhile, soak the glacé fruit in the rum. When the cake is cooked, arrange the fruit on top, allowing the juices to soak into the cake. Sprinkle the top with the sugar and return to the oven for about twenty minutes.
Allow to cool on a wire rack. This cake keeps well for up to a month.

BÛCHE DE NOËL

1½ oz/40 g fine plain flour
1 level tbsp cornflour
1 egg yolk
½ oz/15 g ground almonds
1 level tbsp caster sugar
2 whole eggs
3 oz/75 g caster sugar

Chocolate butter cream
8 oz/200 g granulated sugar
4 fl oz/100 ml water
2 eggs
8 oz/200 g unsalted butter
2 oz/50 g plain chocolate, melted
1 tbsp rum

First make the butter cream.

Measure the water and granulated sugar into a pan and stir over a moderate heat until the sugar has melted.

Boil rapidly until a little syrup, dropped into cold water, forms a soft ball.

While this is cooking, beat the eggs until thick using an electric whisk. Cream the butter until soft.

When the syrup is at the correct temperature, dip the bottom of the pan into cold water to stop the cooking then pour it on to the eggs in a slow stream, beating all the time. Continue to beat until the mixture cools.

Add the butter, a little at a time beating well, then finally, the melted chocolate and rum. Set aside for a few minutes until the cake is ready.

Heat the oven to gas mark 8/230°C/450°F and line a swiss roll tin with non-stick paper.

Sift the flour and cornflour on to a piece of paper.

Mix together the egg yolk, almonds and tbsp of sugar until creamy then add the eggs and remaining sugar and, using an electric mixer, whisk until very thick and creamy.

Sift the flours on to the surface and fold in with a metal spoon.

Turn into the lined tin and bake in the preheated oven for 8 minutes.

Turn out on to a cloth, cover with another cloth and leave to cool for a minute.

Remove the paper and leave to cool under the cloths.

When cool spread with a third of the butter cream and roll up using the cloth to help.

Put the rest of the cream into a piping bag with a fine rose nozzle and pipe the cream in lines down the length of the cake, making wiggles here and there to look like knots in the log.

Dust with cocoa powder and decorated as you wish.

This freezes well.

MARZIPAN STOLLEN

5 fl oz/150 ml milk
2 oz/50 g caster sugar
1 sachet easy blend yeast
12 oz/350 g strong plain flour
4 oz/110 g unsalted butter, softened
1 egg, beaten
3½ oz/90 g currants and sultanas
1 oz/25 g glacé cherries, washed, dried and quartered
1½ oz/40 g read-to-eat dried apricots
1 oz/25 g chopped almonds
a little lemon zest
6 oz/175 g marzipan

Put all the dry ingredients, including the yeast, into a mixing bowl, reserving a little flour.

Warm the milk to blood heat and add to the bowl with the butter and the beaten egg.

Mix everything together until the dough leaves the side of the bowl then turn out on to a floured board and kneed until elastic.

Place in a bowl, covered with plastic film in a warm place until the dough has doubled in size. This may take two hours or even more. Turn the risen dough on to a board sprinkled with the reserved flour and knead lightly again.

Heat the oven to gas mark 5/190°C/375°F.

Roll out the marzipan to form a sausage. Roll out the dough to about 10 ins by 8 ins and place the marzipan on one edge then roll up the dough.

Place on a baking tray and leave to prove for about half an hour.

Bake in a pre-heated oven for 35-40 minutes. Leave to cool a little then lift on to a wire rack.

To finish, mix 4 tbsp icing sugar with a tbsp of lemon juice and spread this over the top of the stollen while still warm.

Perfect Puds

It is a fact of life that, at any gathering, children will devour the savouries, and adults the desserts. I always reckon to make twice as many sweet things for my adult friends as I think I need to. They come in declaring they are on a diet and leave a heap of pudding plates with only crumbs left for the next day. It matters little if the offerings are hot, cold or room temperature, served with cream or custard: if you really want to wow your guests, concentrate on the sweet.

All the best parties have jelly and custard, so I have devised a grown up version for fun. It is based on an old Somerset recipe which is very much in the festive mood while making a cooling change from the heavier sweet things we eat at this time of year.

PORT WINE JELLY WITH CUSTARD TARTLETS

Serves 8

1 pint/600 ml ruby port
2 oz/60 g powdered gelatine
3 oz/90 g white sugar
1/2 pint/300 ml reasonable but not expensive red wine
1 cinnamon stick
juice of 1/2 lemon

Sprinkle the gelatine onto 5 fl oz/150 ml warm water and allow to soak. Then melt by pacing the bowl over hot water. Stir well.
Keeping back half the port, put all the remaining ingredients including the gelatine into a pan and heat until almost boiling. Remove from the heat and pour in the rest of the port. Pour into a dampened mould and leave to set.
To serve, dip quickly into hot water and place a plate over the mould, up-end the two and the jelly should come away cleanly.
Surround the jelly with tiny tartlet cases, baked blind. To do this, use scrunched up foil. When cool fill them with a spoonful of confectioners, or ordinary thick, custard flavoured with a little liqueur, and top with a whirl of cinnamon flavoured cream.

CHOCOLATE AND ORANGE CHEESECAKE

Serves 6-8

12 bourbon biscuits, finely crushed
5 oz/150 g butter, melted

Filling
½ lb/225 g low fat cottage cheese
½ lb/225 g ricotta or cream cheese
2 oz/50 g caster sugar
juice of half a lemon
a few drops vanilla essence
½ pint/300 ml single cream
1 tbsp gelatine
3 oz/75 g dessert chocolate
1 tin mandarin oranges in juice, drained

Mix the crushed biscuits with the butter and press on to the base and sides of an oiled 8 inch/20 cm loose-bottomed cake tin. Chill until firm.

To make the filling: sieve the cottage cheese into a mixing bowl. Add the ricotta or cream cheese and mix with a wooden spoon until combined.

Add the sugar, lemon juice, vanilla and cream and mix well.

Sprinkle the gelatine over 3 tbsp water, leave to soak then melt by placing the bowl over hot water and stir until dissolved. Leave to cool slightly then stir into the cheese mixture.

Melt the chocolate.

Pour the cheese mixture into the crust, then drizzle the melted chocolate over the surface and swirl in with the point of a skewer to create a marbled effect. Cover and chill for at least three hours.

To serve, run a knife around the edge of the crust and release the sides of the tin. Slide on to a serving plate. Decorate the edge with the orange segments. This cake freezes well for up to a month.

In the 'olden days' most households relied upon the calorific value of steamed and baked puds to supply their basic energy requirements. Meat has always been expensive, so puddings were used to ensure the family left the table feeling satisfied. Of course, less was known about the benefits of a diet higher in fibre and protein and lower in fat and sugar. In these days of relative affluence and convenience foods the sheer bliss of a little self indulgence is sometimes forgotten.

BANANA AND CHOC CHIP PUDDING

2 oz/60 g margarine
2 oz/60 g caster sugar
4 oz/120 g self-raising flour
1 egg
1 tbsp milk
2 tbsp plain chocolate chips
1 banana, chopped

Cream the margarine and sugar until pale.
Fold in the flour, alternating with the beaten egg and milk.
Fold in the banana and chocolate.
Butter a pint basin and spoon the mixture into it. Cover with greaseproof paper and foil.
Steam for 1½ hours and serve with custard sauce.

REAL CUSTARD

1 pint/600 ml milk
4 egg yolks
2 tbsp caster sugar
vanilla pod or a few drops real vanilla essence
2 tsp arrowroot

Heat the milk to boiling point with the vanilla.

Meanwhile, beat the egg yolks with the sugar until pale and thick. Stir in the arrowroot.

Add the strained hot milk whisking well then return to the pan and cook over boiling water (or in a double saucepan) until the custard coats the back of a spoon. The arrowroot is not essential but it prevents the custard from curdling should it get too hot. If you do not wish to serve it immediately, leave it over the hot water, off the stove and cover the surface with a piece of damp greaseproof paper to prevent a skin from forming.

INDEX

NOTES

NOTES

Cooking on Gas ...with love

Many of the world's leading chefs will tell you, nothing can hold a candle to gas for sheer 'controllability'. The flame is fast and responsive, springing up or subsiding instantaneously, at just the turn of a control.

Joan Bunting enjoys cooking on gas, and you could too. Simply call into your local Gas showroom to see the very latest in cookers with exciting new features, offering economy and versatility. They turn cooking into a pleasure.

British Gas
Northern

CP PRINTING & PUBLISHING LIMITED

Kellaw Road, Yarm Road Industrial Estate, Darlington, Co. Durham DL1 4YA
Telephone: Darlington (0325) 382360